GW01402988

Making Connections

Promoting attachments between parents and carers and their young children

by
Dr Hannah Mortimer

Acknowledgements
With acknowledgements to Brompton House Child and Family Centre, Northallerton; to colleagues at SureStart Stockton-on-Tees; and to my friend and mentor, Heather Bacon.

Q✓
Ed

A QEd Publication

Published in 2006

© Hannah Mortimer

ISBN 1 898873 47 X

British Library Cataloguing
A catalogue record for this book is available from the British Library.

$$\boxed{\begin{array}{c} Q\checkmark \\ Ed \end{array}}$$

Published by QEd Publications, 39 Weeping Cross, Stafford ST17 0DG
Tel: 01785 620364
Fax: 01785 607797
Web site: www.qed.uk.com
Email: orders@qed.uk.com

Printed in the United Kingdom by Stowes (Stoke-on-Trent).

Contents

Introduction

The aim of the series

This series is for those working in Sure Start centres and other early years practitioners who want to work with parents or carers of young children in groups. In recent years, there has been a blossoming of Sure Start schemes all over the country with massive recruitment and intensive staff training as more and more schemes come on line. Even after the first flush of schemes, there will be new and strengthened children's centres and community services that continue in their place. These books have been put together by practitioners who already have parent and carer groups up and running. They are the result of trying out approaches and evaluating their success and the hope is that they will provide practical ideas for colleagues starting new groups to prevent them having to reinvent the wheel. Inevitably, you will each be serving very individual communities with particular sets of needs, but it is hoped that you will find plenty of ideas in this series that will get you started.

Making Connections groups are a helpful way of working with parents or carers who have attachment difficulties with their young children. The benefits of working in *groups* with parents or carers of young children are to promote friendship and mutual support; reduce isolation; help children develop social and language skills; and help adults share information and advice in a palatable and non-threatening manner.

Since the daily work of many Sure Start schemes is centred around family support and since this so often occurs in groups or 'drop-ins' held at a Sure Start base or children's centre, these books are about how you make that delicate move from the informal 'drop-in' to the kind of structure that will enable you to improve confidences, relationships and quality of communications between parents or carers and their children under five.

The series includes books on:

RUMPUS Groups	behaviour management groups for parents or carers and their young children.
Step by Step Groups	groups that provide ideas and support to parents or carers to enable them to encourage their child's development (if the child is vulnerable or might have SEN).
Music and Play Groups	groups that provide circle time and structured play activities that improve relationships between parents or carers and their children.
Baby and Me	parent groups that promote early development, relationships and communication in their babies.
Making Connections	therapeutic groups for parents or carers to help them form stronger attachments with their children.

Sure Start

In Sure Start schemes, families are targeted to receive information, support and guidance to help them make the most of their young child's developmental, learning and social potential, and also to improve upon their parenting and child-rearing skills. The aim is to improve the life chances of young children in areas of 'risk' through improving their access to education, health services, family support and advice on nurturing. Typical Sure Start schemes provide a range of services and provision – there might be outreach and home visiting; support to families; opportunities for quality play, learning and childcare experiences for young children; advice on child and family health; and support for families who have a young child with special educational needs (SEN) or a disability. Even after the first rounds of funding for Sure Start, the aim is for the work to continue and to develop within local children's centres.

What is a Making Connections group?

These groups were based on the *Relationship Play* approach developed by a team of professionals in the north east (Binney, McKnight and Broughton, 1994) at Sheffield Children's Hospital and in Doncaster NHS Trust. The author had worked with this model in the Northallerton NHS Trust under the title 'Hugs and Tugs' along with her psychology colleague, Heather Bacon. This book owes much to the professionals and families who attended the groups at that time.

In 'attachment' terms (see further details later), the groups aim to provide a secure base, a shared narrative and a constructive session for parents to explore and develop the relationship that they have with their young children. In this book, you will read about all these approaches and the model is now offered as part of the menu of provision in some Sure Start schemes.

Each group has six parent and child pairs who come for ten sessions on a weekly basis. We have found it essential to invite parents who are all of the same gender – mother and child pairs – though see no reason why we could not use the model with father and child pairs if we had a cohort of six who needed this kind of help. The term 'mothers' will be used throughout this book since most of our groups have centred around mother and child 'diads' (or pairs). There is usually one particular child in the family identified as needing a stronger relationship with one particular parent, though other siblings under school age attend a crèche that runs parallel to the group. We will use the term 'mothers' to imply either a parent or a carer. We will use the term 'child' to refer to the child in the mother-child pair for whom the intervention is targeted.

What actually happens?

As the families arrive, they are greeted and served with refreshments in a crèche room. Once the children have settled a little and any babies are occupied by the crèche workers, the mothers withdraw with three 'therapists' into a more intimate room for an hour's talking and sharing. All sorts of issues are covered, ranging from how difficult it is to be a mum to everyone's hopes for the future and how they wish to change things. There are ground rules for confidentiality and an atmosphere of trust and sharing is established. After the hour, the mothers and therapists move into a third room where there is a carpeted floor space. Here they are joined by those children whom the group is trying to support – in other words, there are now six mother and child pairs. Other children in the family (where there are not the same worries about relationships) remain in the crèche. A series of relationship play games are then shared by the mother and child pairs. These are graded week by week so that they become more physical and intimate as the mothers and children become more focused on each other and more able to accept and give physical contact and emotional nurture. This takes a further 15 minutes or so. The mothers then collect any other siblings from the crèche and say their farewells.

How to use this book

You now have an overview of what a Making Connections group might look like. Here is an outline of what to expect in the book:

- In the first chapter, you will consider when and why you might like to run such a group and how it might fit into the Sure Start framework of provision, or indeed into the community service that you offer.

- Chapter 2 helps you plan ahead – what you need in terms of equipment, personnel, premises and skills.

- In Chapter 3 there are suggestions for the mothers' group at the beginning of the session.

- In Chapter 4 there are suggestions for the relationship play activities or 'play time' at the end of the group.

- Chapter 5 contains suggestions for evaluation and reporting back to management committees.

- Finally, there are some helpful resources and contacts listed at the back.

Throughout the book there are ideas and suggestions from practitioners who have actually developed and run these groups. These should help you to understand why certain approaches were used and what the particular challenges and opportunities were in running the groups.

Chapter 1

Why have a Making Connections group?

In the first chapter we cover *when* and *why* you might like to run such a group and how it might fit into the Sure Start framework of provision, or indeed into the more general early years service that you offer.

One of our prime reasons for developing Making Connections groups was to improve the relationships between parents or carers and their children, especially where professionals or the parents themselves were identifying difficulties – in other words, to promote positive attachments. From research, we now know more about patterns of attachment between parents and their children and we can begin to separate those who are successfully 'connected' or 'bonded' from those who are not. One manager and health visitor, Karen Bibbings, has devised this simple activity to explain what 'connection' looks like.

The Glums

Below is a scenario that could be used as a staff discussion point.

Imagine you are sitting in a restaurant. In one corner, there is a couple who are obviously deeply in love. We will call them 'the Lovers'. How do you *know* that they are in love? What behaviours do you actually observe? Make a list of these on a large sheet of paper.

Now imagine you are in the same restaurant and in another corner is a couple who are clearly not getting on very well. We will call them 'the Glums'. What do you actually see or hear this time? Make another list.

Things to consider:
- Think about parents or carers and children who are 'attached' or 'connected' to each other. Do you observe similar behaviours as 'the Lovers' and 'the Glums'?

- You now know what a connected child and carer look like. Can you also recognise when such a connection is not there?

- Think of ways you can support attachments/connections by helping parents or carers 'tune in' to their children and to share pleasure in each other.

From an activity by Karen Bibbings, former Health Visitor,
Stockton-on-Tees SureStart (with permission)

Patterns of attachment

There are some children whose challenging behaviour is very resistant to change. These are the children who can settle better if given 'secure attachment figures' to relate to who can support, offer consistency of handling, and be there to reassure and to encourage. Attachment Theory argues that children develop a style of relating to important attachment figures in their lives, which secures for them the best parenting available under the circumstances.

The study of attachments has opened up a whole new way of assessing family relationships and providing therapeutic support. The patterns of attachment remain remarkably consistent over time until the child is about six and so can be observed, identified and worked with. Many of these parents find that their pre-school children are difficult to control, extremely angry and aggressive, or highly anxious and 'clingy'. Therapists might have tried to teach them behavioural management techniques, but where there is an attachment difficulty, the behaviour tends to persist, partly because the emotional climate and the relationships are not conducive to change.

Where attachment is working securely, an infant's cries and demands will be met reliably with sensitivity and warmth by the carer, and the growing child develops in confidence and independence. We know this because of the influential research of John Bowlby (1988) and colleagues into bonding, attachment and loss. If a parent is unresponsive or rejects their cries of distress, that child may act as if independent long before he or she is emotionally ready to be. The child might pay little attention when the parent leaves them at nursery and seldom look at the parent or try to involve them in play. This is known as a pattern of 'anxious-avoidant' attachment.

If a parent is inconsistent in responding, perhaps because of periods of depression or frequent absences, the child learns to cry or shout louder with their demands, producing a pattern of 'ambivalent' attachment. There is also a pattern of 'disorganised' or 'controlling' attachment in which children develop a very controlling style over their parent in order to maintain some degree of predictability or structure in their lives. This pattern is common with parents who might have suffered loss, trauma or abuse themselves, or lack a 'secure base' of their own from which to provide nurture and care to others in their lives. Understanding about attachments does not mean that we should go forth and proclaim that a parent or child 'has an attachment disorder'. However, it does help us to understand that there is an emotional component to the behaviour or the relationship which may involve us trying to intervene on an emotional level as well as a behavioural or teaching level.

We know that children with a positive self-image are likely to be more independent, better socially adjusted, more likely to achieve academically. We also know that children who have warm, affectionate relationships with their parents usually have high self-esteem. Therefore it makes sense to plan Sure Start interventions to improve the relationship between parents or carers and their children in order to gain all the benefits of higher self-esteem. Children who have high self-esteem show improved learning, behaviour, independence, confidence, relationships and motivation. They are able to accept criticism or failure without giving up or becoming defensive and they value and respect themselves as individuals. On the other hand, children with low self-esteem have a strong need for reassurance and praise from others. They tend to feel insecure, lack trust in their own competence and have a low opinion of themselves. They have problems in trying out new experiences or in learning and a tendency to over-react to failure.

When you consider that a relationship needs two sides – parent and child – and that either can be affected by low self-esteem, you can understand how important it is to design interventions that aim to improve the self-esteem of both parents and children. Making Connections is one attempt to do so.

Theoretical background

What are the theoretical underpinnings of a Making Connections group? There are two key texts: Holmes (1993) and Binney, McKnight and Broughton (1994) and you will find full references on page 48. Holmes reviewed what we know about Attachment Theory and argued that we could use this knowledge to plan therapeutic interventions for families where attachments were not working securely.

The main features of attachment theory that have emerged from research are these. We know from research of birds and monkeys that the mother-infant relationship is not led by the need to feed alone but by the need for protection, and this seems to cause infants to seek close proximity to their carers. Once an infant is close, then it is as if it has a 'secure base' from which to explore and find out. In other words, proximity leads to security and learning. If one separates infant from carer, there is a 'separation protest', the purpose of which is to gain a reunion. If this protest does not bring the carer back, the infant is less likely to explore and can even, in certain circumstances, become 'frozen'. This was very clear when researchers began to study young children isolated in hospital in the days when parents and carers were not allowed to stay with them.

Attachments continue to develop throughout life, particularly at key life stages such as adolescence and partnership, and adult attachments and relationships are influenced by earlier ones. Bowlby (1988) was the first to draw together all these findings in the late fifties and early sixties.

Holmes argues that, with this knowledge, we can design therapy to support families who are not securely attached. The research points towards making use of certain key aspects when designing interventions and these have been incorporated into the design of Making Connections groups:

Providing a secure base

Just as 'good' parents provide a secure base for their child from which to explore and learn, the therapists need to provide a sense of security when planning their work with the families. There needs to be consistency, regularity, reliability and the combination of warmth with firm boundaries. The non-verbal behaviour of the therapists needs to suggest that they are in tune with the mother.

Using a shared narrative

Therapists and mother together need to develop a shared story about what is happening in the family, finding words that make sense to both of them. Being able (and having the time and space) to tell your own story is very helpful when working on family relationships and attachments.

Recognising and managing feelings

Strong and basic emotions are sometimes aroused and these need to be contained by the therapists and managed with calm, warmth and clear boundaries.

Thinking about what is happening

There is also a clear role for spending time thinking about what is happening and what triggers certain events within the family. This comes from Bowlby's (1988) idea that children developed 'internal working models' of themselves, their carers and their relationships which influenced how they behaved. It also borrows from a very successful intervention called 'cognitive behaviour therapy' in which clients think about patterns in their behaviour and reactions in order to challenge and change them.

The strange situation test

Mary Ainsworth first devised a method of assessing attachments in the late sixties. She called this the 'strange situation' test and it is used as part of the assessment during a Making Connections group.

If a parent and young toddler are settled together in a playroom and the mother then leaves for a short spell (about three minutes), an observer might see one of three things happen:

- The secure child protests and then protests again when she reappears, though is easily pacified.

- The insecure-avoidant child does not protest when she leaves and hovers when she returns, unable to play freely.

- The insecure-ambivalent child protests and cannot be pacified on her return, clinging and refusing any toys or comfort.

- The insecure-disorganised child seems to freeze on separation and seems unable to behave in an organised way.

Training courses are now available for using Attachment Theory in specialist assessment by such professionals as Pat Crittenden. We used the model in our own more general way as a sign of whether attachments were improving in the group. There is a moment at the beginning and end of the mothers' group when mothers and children separate and reunite and we always delegated one person to observe one of the diads and make notes of their reactions.

The development of Relationship Play

Building on the work of Bowlby, Ainsworth and others, Binney, McKnight and Broughton (1994) described a new form of group therapy for mother-child pairs with serious attachment disturbances. It was developed by members of the Doncaster Family Psychiatry Team to assist children of four to seven years and was based on Attachment Theory. Their programme lasted over 12 weeks and had as its core a Play Therapy session and a Mothers' Talk Group. The play session used 'desensitisation' to gradually help mothers feel more confident and emotionally available to their children when playing closely and when in physical contact. Weeks one to three consisted of light group games with mothers, children and professionals. Weeks four to seven had the addition of light paired games with mother and child pairs. Weeks eight to twelve had the addition of more intimate paired games.

The Talk group enabled mothers to explore the feelings that the play therapy aroused as well as to link current difficulties with children and adults to their own childhood experiences. Though not a panacea for all attachment problems, evaluations were most positive and mothers seem to have found the groups helpful. Video recordings of mothers and children playing together before and after the sessions showed clear improvements for many. Others required more intensive or individual follow-up. The authors' eventual goal was for longer-term self-help or community support systems to maintain and support the changes obtained in the groups. This, too, is the aim of offering a Making Connections group within a wider Sure Start menu of provision.

Which families benefit most from Making Connections?

We have found that Making Connections groups are most effective for:

- Parent and child pairs where the parents have reached the point of deciding that 'things have got to change'. They may not have linked this to the need to become better attached to their child, but this has not mattered.

- Parents with low self-esteem and confidence, perhaps relating to their own experiences of being parented.

- Parents who wish to improve their relationship with one particular child.

- Parents who are saddened by how negative their relationship with their child has become.

- Parents looking for the 'good times' of day-to-day parenting.

We have not found Making Connections groups helpful for:

- Parents who have significant mental health problems.

- Families who are *told* to attend rather than who choose to.

- Parents who have a significant history of being abused that has not yet been worked on. Where this fact is discovered during the course of the group, it is important to arrange other therapeutic help for that mother where past issues can be explored more confidentially and supportively – Making Connections may be a later stage for her.

We have found Making Connections to be just as effective for children with all levels of ability, regardless of disability or special need. In that respect, it is an inclusive provision. We also found that it fitted most easily where there was a whole scaffold of support – for example, antenatal care groups; post-natal support groups; services and groups to support those with post-natal depression; Music and Play groups (for building relationships and learning to play together); RUMPUS (for toddler behaviour difficulties); and Making Connections (for more entrenched attachment difficulties). You will find that there is further information on some of these groups in other books in this series (see page 48).

Making Connections in Sure Start

Here is an example of how Making Connections might fit into a Sure Start framework of provision. In SureStart Stockton-on-Tees, there are many schemes serving urban and diverse communities. We saw it as fitting into a wider framework of provision in which parents or carers fell into three main categories:

- Hard to reach – they need support but may not ask for it or even want it.

- Mainstream – they both need and want support.

- Easy to reach – they probably do not really need support but want it anyway.

We decided that, within the Sure Start philosophy, provision should be offered inclusively to all these categories and that it should be available at three stages of family life:

- Bump Club – prenatal support.

- New Arrivals – early days of parenting.

- Parent/carer and toddler – the pre-school years.

This kind of thinking enables one to draw up a grid of support, making sure that each category of parent has access to support at different family life stages. For the 'hard-to-reach' families, you might opt for a home visiting model as a first stage towards involving that family in more group-based activity and support. We saw Making Connections as fitting into the framework for supporting 'mainstream' and 'hard-to-reach' families at the parent/carer and toddler stages. In other words, Making Connections sessions are helpful for parents or carers who want to improve their relationship with their child and who need high-level support from their health visitor or Sure Start worker.

Chapter 2

Planning ahead

Chapter 2 helps you plan ahead – what you need in terms of equipment, personnel, premises and skills. Suppose you have a cohort of several families for whom you would like to plan a Making Connections group. This is what you need to do next.

Informing colleagues

You have a decision to make right at the beginning. Will you accept open referrals from any family who wishes to be included, or will you only accept referrals from other professionals? The first would allow you to be utterly inclusive but might lead to your providing a very costly and staff-intensive resource for those who 'want it, but may not need it'. You might also be missing those hard-to-reach families who would really benefit. In practice, if your local service has developed to the point where a wide range of clients are already accessing your services and are well informed about what you have on offer and why, you might offer a combination of these approaches. Decide what your referral criteria will be and allow families to self-refer on the understanding that you will then approach other professionals to make sure they meet your criteria.

To give you an idea of the sort of approaches you might make to other professional colleagues, here is an example. It is a copy of a letter to colleagues that one service decided to send out before starting their Making Connections group.

Dear colleague

Making Connections

It has come to our attention that many of the families with children under five that we work with share similar difficulties. We have identified that a number of the mothers and children have relationship/attachment difficulties. To meet this need we are hoping to set up a 'relationship play' group which we are calling **Making Connections**. The approaches we shall use are based on Attachment Theory.

What it will involve

It will involve weekly attendance for six mothers and identified children (one child per parent) over ten weeks. There will be two parallel groups: one for the mothers and therapists to explore issues in relationships and a crèche facility for the children and any siblings under school age who need to come too. At the end of each session will be a relationship play time in which mother and child pairs engage in carefully graded play activities to develop their relationship together.

Referral criteria

1. Child's age under five

2. Mother and child are experiencing poor emotional bonding

3. One child per mother to be worked with

4. Maximum six pairs per group

5. Referrals in writing please to: (contact details)

If you wish to discuss specific pairs prior to referral, please do not hesitate to contact us.

Yours sincerely

cc. Health visitors, social workers, Sure Start managers, early years education support team.

Here is an example of a flyer that was available in health centres and Sure Start settings as one way of making the services on offer transparent and accessible to all.

Making Connections

We know that children behave better and families feel happier when relationships are working well. We are starting a group for mothers who wish to improve their relationship with one of their children under five.

Contact your local health visitor or Sure Start worker if you are interested in attending. They will then refer you to us with further information to make sure we are the best group to help you.

Where?   Grange Family Centre
When?   Friday mornings for 10 weeks
Time?   09.30a.m. to 11.00a.m.

What happens?

09.30am   Meet, drinks and snacks.
09.45am   Mums meet togethor in their own group while their children are looked after in the crèche.
10.45am   A special play time in which mums are helped to share
fun   with the child they want to work with, following special exercises and activities. Any brothers or sisters stay in the crèche so that mums can enjoy a special time together with just one of their children.
11.00am   Finish.

All ten sessions need to be attended to gain the best benefit.

For more information, contact: Grange Sure Start Office

Finding rooms

Finding the right suite of rooms for this kind of group can be challenging, but has become much easier since the development of Sure Start Centres and Children's Centres. We have also used Social Services Family Centres and Health Centres. You need:

- a crèche room with the usual facilities for the children;

- a medium-sized room with clear floor space for the relationship play session;

- a meeting room with a circle of comfortable chairs for the mothers' group, together with flip chart or similar;

- refreshment facilities.

All of these need to be close together and preferably within the same suite of rooms.

Inviting the families

You are unlikely to have a whole cohort of families with both the needs and the willingness together at one time. In practice, some services meet regularly to plan their groups and services for the next term or so, and it is at these meetings that names are suggested for a group such as Making Connections. You might end up with one or two groups a year.

Before putting names of mother and child couples forward, the professional involved needs to have made sure that they meet the referral criteria, would benefit from this kind of group, are fully informed that this is being discussed for them and willing to give it a try.

Once the group has been agreed, this is the kind of letter that services send out to prospective clients:

A follow-up visit or chat from someone who knows the family well is
invaluable in moving the selection forward and reassuring or informing
those who have been invited.

Collecting video data

If you are evaluating your service, then you will need to plan how this will
be done. When these kinds of groups were first set up and evaluated (and
there was a long-term project at Sheffield Children's Hospital to do this),
video evidence of mother and child playing together was used to provide
qualitative evidence of any change in relationship. For professionals who
have received specialist training in assessing attachments, the video data
can be used in a more finely tuned way. Below is an example of how one
service recorded and evaluated its data.

It was decided to video parent and child together for 10 minutes before the
group began and again at its end. The videos were recorded in the family's
own home, with their agreement. It was felt that families should be entitled

to decline if they so wished. This is the kind of letter that was sent. About two-thirds of the families agreed to being filmed, especially when the service offered to give them a tape of their child afterwards.

Dear

We are looking forward to seeing you and . . . . at the Making Connections group.

As part of this, it would be very helpful if we could see how . . . . is playing and behaving with you at present and how this changes over the sessions.

If you are willing, I would like to visit you at home to video 10 minutes of play before the group starts. I can repeat this at the end of the sessions. It might be interesting for you to keep the video at the end and see whether things have changed.

I can also use this visit to tell you a little more about the group and talk about your hopes for it.

If you are at all worried about being video recorded with your child, please let me know and we need not do so. I look forward to visiting you on (date, time). Please let me know if this is not convenient by contacting me at . . . .

Yours sincerely

The video was set up in the following way. The sitting room was used and a selection of simple toys was brought by the filmer – a few picture books, a simple train set, a teddy and bed, an inset shape board and a toy tea service. Mother and child were invited to explore the box together on the floor. The filmer reassured the mother that the filming would focus on how the child responded and played rather than on her. She was asked to play and interact in the way she normally would. Towards the end (to a pre-arranged signal), she was asked to leave the room briefly while the filmer reassured and talked to the child. After two minutes or so she was to return to the room. Thus the video footage contained a record of the play interaction as well as a response to a 'strange situation' and separation (see page 15).

This was repeated at the end of the ten group sessions and the video was analysed by a clinical psychologist specialised in working with attachments. It is also possible to carry out a simpler (though cruder) qualitative assessment by observing:

- whether the mother talks to her child or remains silent;

- whether she directs the child or is able to follow her child's interests;

- how much they look at each other;

- how well they listen to each other and adjust what they are doing;

- how much they interact;

- how much they appear to be enjoying each other;

- ratio of positive to negative comments;

- how the child reacts on separation;

- how the child reacts on being reunited.

Refreshments

You might decide to offer drinks on arrival when mothers deliver their children to the crèche. Certainly it is helpful for them to take their drinks with them as they join the mothers' group. Some groups offer refreshments at the end when the families are all reunited at the end of the relationship play time. You will, of course, need to follow your usual safety regulations concerning mixing hot drinks and young children together in the same place.

Staffing

Crèche workers

This will depend on how many children attend. Although the group is for mother and child pairs, there are likely to be other siblings not yet at school to be cared for. Once you know the numbers, you will need crèche workers to your usual ratios for the ages and stages involved. There is no reason at all why the children joining the crèche should not be included in an existing crèche already running in that building for other children.

Group therapists

You need three professionals to run the mothers' group:

- The main therapist should be an experienced therapist, perhaps a clinical/educational psychologist, an experienced social/family worker or other group/family therapist. This person should have experience both of working with attachments and also within therapeutic groups.

- One person should be co-therapist. This person might be a social worker or family worker, senior Sure Start worker, health visitor, psychologist or someone else who has experience of family work.

- A third person should be observer. Their role is not to participate but to be aware of the dynamics and themes covered within the group so that feedback can be given later to the two therapists with suggestions for how they will steer the group the following session. This person can either be very experienced (also playing a training and supervision role) or could be a therapist-in-training or psychologist.

Relationship play leader

This person is likely also to be one of the professionals in the mothers' group. He or she will need to have experience in playing with parents and young children in a group setting. One group used an educational psychologist who also had nursery teaching experience and was a musician. Another used an occupational therapist who had experience in play therapy. Another used a senior play facilitator. Confidence to lead and facilitate the group is as important as experience here.

You will find it helpful to draw up a planning sheet detailing your clients and your staffing.

Making Connections
Planning sheet
Confidential

Venue: _____   Time of group: _____

	Mums invited	Child's name	Age	Other sibling(s) for crèche	Age(s)
1.					
2.					
3.					
4.					
5.					
6.					

Staffing Rota

	Date	Mums' group (2)	Observer (1)	Crèche (?)	Play time leader (1)
1.					
2.					
3.					
4.					
5.					
6.					
7.					
8.					
9.					
10.					

Planning your time

To give you an idea of the timescale involved, below is an example of a timetable for the group.

Timetable	
9.00a.m.	Professionals arrive and prepare.
9.30a.m.	Families arrive, are greeted and served with refreshments in a crèche room.
9.40a.m.	Separation: once the children have settled a little and any babies are occupied by the crèche workers, the mothers withdraw with three 'therapists' into a more intimate room.
9.45a.m.	Mothers' group: mothers, therapists and observer start their group.
10.45a.m.	Play time: Mothers and therapists move into a third room where there is a carpeted floor space. Here they are joined by just those children whom the group is trying to support – in other words, there are now mother and child pairs (children in the family where there are not the same worries about relationships remain in the crèche).
11.00a.m.	Mothers collect siblings from the crèche and say their farewells.
11.00–11.30a.m.	Therapist, co-therapist, observer and senior crèche worker(s) meet for feedback and to plan the next session.

Booking crèche equipment

Your service will already be familiar with the range of toys and facilities needed for providing a crèche and most Sure Start schemes will have a crèche co-ordinator who can assist you in this part of the planning. Take the trouble to find out a little bit about the children who will be attending and what their particular needs and interests are. The kind of crèche activity provided for a Making Connections group is identical to any other crèche – in other words, this is not a therapeutic group in the sense that the mothers' group and the relationship play time are.

Transport

Depending on your location, you might find yourselves considering the need for additional transport arrangements for some of your families attending. Sometimes it might be possible to arrange for a mother to join a special minibus service already arranged in connection with a crèche or out-of-school service.

Chapter 3

Talking time

This chapter focuses on the therapy session at the beginning of the group and provides many suggestions.

An individual approach

When we first started running this kind of group, we looked eagerly for a prescriptive list of what we should cover on each session but, quite rightly, this was not available. What you cover and how you cover it will depend on the group of mothers you are working with. If you were too prescriptive and followed a 'map' too closely, you would not be available to respond flexibly to the needs of the group and you would not be listening reflectively. This is where your observer comes in – he or she should have picked up the small comment or 'atmosphere' that could suggest where you travel next in the following session. Unless you are extremely experienced and confident, it is difficult to both hold a therapeutic conversation and also pick up every nuance from each member of the group. This is why three of you are needed. The *therapeutic* nature of the group comes from the fact that you are not following a set script or pre-designed 'course' but you are going where you need to go with your particular clients and their needs. This chapter therefore covers places you might like to travel to, rather than prescribing the particular route or itinerary you use.

Necessary beginnings

In the first session you are going to need more structure than in the others. This is because you must cover the ground rules (especially of confidentiality) at this stage and set the scene for the rest of the sessions. You will find it helpful to have a flip chart and pens available to record ground rules so that you can later stick this on the wall to remind yourselves at later sessions. We always arrange the chairs in a circle so that we can share information together and communicate more clearly as a group. The professionals are part of this circle and not seated away from the parents in any sense. The group lasts from 50 minutes to an hour, finishing promptly so that children could join mothers for the relationship play time. Here are some of the things to cover during the first session.

Introductions

We found it helpful to introduce ourselves very much as people first and what our role was second. In other words, the professionals started the process off by an informal introduction along the lines:

Hello. My name is Gina – Gina D . . . and I am also one of the people who will be leading the group. I work as a (job role) at (base) and I cover the (locality) area of the town. I have experience in working with families mostly with children under five and this is my first Making Connections group.

The mothers, in turn, give us their names and tell us about their children. They also say a few words about why they come to the group. This should not be too threatening since they will already have had a home visit and have talked about this before.

When it is the turn of the observer, he or she makes an effort to be as warm and friendly as possible at this point, in order to make themselves as unthreatening as possible. We used a script something like this:

Hello, My name is Fiona and I am also a (job role). My job in this group is different from the rest. I am not going to take part in the group, but am going to listen very carefully so that I can advise my colleagues later how best to help you all. I might notice things that the rest of you have missed and ideas might occur to me. That is why you will see me writing notes. Please remember that I am not studying you all! I am simply writing things down as they occur to me so that I can support my colleagues in their work later. And although you will find me sitting silently in the group, I look forward to chatting to you over coffee each week when you all arrive, and sharing the play time with you at the end of the session. I shall now keep quiet, but wish you all the best for your time in the group.

The purpose of the group

The therapist then outlines the purpose of the group. He or she will describe how all of the mothers present have said that they want to work on their relationship with one particular child. The link between having a good relationship with your child and helping them look, listen and behave well will be made (this licenses the mother to talk about difficult behaviour later on).

You can make the point that children do not come with manuals and it can be really helpful to realise they are not on their own – that there are many others who are 'going through it' too. Make the point that the professionals do not have all the answers, but they might be able to make suggestions that will help. Highlight the fact that some of the best ideas may come from listening to each other. Explain that research has shown that just having time to talk about your own life, what things were like when you were little and what your feelings about parenting are, can actually help the process of bonding more closely with your child. Explain that good bonding and attachment makes parenting more pleasurable and prevents you having to constantly nag and be negative.

Say a little about the structure of each session. Explain that, at the end of the mothers' group, you will be moving into another room where the children the mothers are working with will join you for some special games that have proved helpful in improving relationships. Reassure them that although these might be a little embarrassing at first, they will soon get used to them, especially when they see the children enjoying them and behaving so well.

Ground rules

Put these out for discussion, but steer the ideas towards the following:

Punctuality and attendance
Make a real point of being on time for the start of the session. Encourage everyone to share transport difficulties with you. You should already have planned the start to fit in with dropping off times for any siblings at local

schools. Any unexpected absence should be followed by a phone call to whoever is identified to co-ordinate attendance. If anyone misses more than two sessions, they will have to leave the group. If the absences could not be helped, you can always try to include that family in a future group.

Confidentiality

Agree that everything said within the group should be kept completely confidential. Nothing discussed inside the group should be talked about outside the group. Point out that everyone must feel safe about sharing things with each other, safe in the knowledge that it will not be gossiped about. Point out the exceptions to confidentiality as well. The first is that the observer will be discussing what has gone on within the group with the other professionals later and that this will be done professionally and confidentially. Point out, too, that professionals are bound to disclose any information relating to a child's safety or criminal act to the appropriate authorities. If this is not stated clearly right at the beginning, you might find yourselves in an impossible 'double bind' later. Child protection procedures are always paramount.

Respect for each other

You might wish to cover matters such as 'no put-downs', 'we will turn off mobile phones' and 'we will listen to each other with respect'. Try to use the words that your clients offer.

Your children are safe

We also cover an issue to do with the children's happiness. Since some mothers are very anxious about leaving their children in the crèche (and this is in the nature of an anxious attachment), we undertook that a crèche worker would come and tell them if at any point their child needed them. We hoped that this would help them abdicate their emotional responsibility for their child for the duration of the group.

Starting points

We tend to start with a round of 'what it's like for me' in which each group member talks about what is most difficult with their child. Therapist an join in with this too if it is appropriate in your case. This gives us a starting point in terms of what the most difficult issues are for our clients. We list issues (in general terms) on the flip chart – temper tantrums, going out, night-times – ready to revisit at a later session.

The co-therapist works hard to bring other mothers in or to reflect an issue back to someone else: 'Did you find that as well?' 'That's how you said you felt too, isn't it?' 'Is that the same for all of you?' That way, one member who speaks a lot can have their statements respected yet helped to give others a turn. This takes up most of the first session. We finish with a round of what the best bit of parenting is. Even if a member cannot think of one thing, we suggest how hard they are trying because they are coming to the group. Thus we aim to end on a positive note.

Feedback from the observer

At the end of the session, when the families have all gone home, professionals from both the mothers' group and senior crèche worker(s) meet together for half-an-hour's feedback. It is helpful to have a senior crèche worker present, so that she or he can provide information on a child's behaviour and reactions in the crèche which help the other professionals make sense of a mother's behaviour or reactions in the group.

Sometimes, for example, a mother will paint a very dark picture of her child's behaviour when talking in the group, yet the crèche workers will have found a beautifully responsive child in the crèche. This, again, can be in the nature of an attachment difficulty. The observer will read back notes, reminding the therapists of what ground was covered. The observer might point out that one of the mothers was looking particularly angry, worried or anxious at one point and that there were clearly things to explore further in that respect.

Each week, the therapists and observer each undertake to observe a child and mother pair at the point of separating before the mother's group and re-uniting after the group. This again will be discussed in the feedback meeting, the aim being to see a more 'normal' pattern by the end of the sessions.

The crèche workers might also be reporting on how well a child settled or behaved in the group and a description of behaviour will help the other therapists narrow down on the issues they are dealing with. Out of this half-hour's discussion comes a plan for the next session – how many crèche workers will be needed, any particular toys useful for the crèche, any particular activities useful for the play time and what direction the next mothers' group will take. The following suggestions are only that – suggestions for different areas you might cover depending on where your group is going and how fast it is 'getting there'.

Suggestions

Becoming a mum

Spend time talking about pregnancy and birth. You will find that some denied the fact of the pregnancy or found that it got in the way of things. Others might have felt overwhelmed. Others too will have had high hopes and aspirations dashed by the practicalities of having to look after a baby. Others too will have had, or still have, post-natal depression. This is something to discuss in the feedback session and observe further. Someone who knows the mother well could then follow this up with her separately, leading, perhaps, to a referral to an appropriate professional if further help is needed. Talk about pregnancy and birth usually generates a lot of interest and sharing and is a useful topic to cover early in the sessions.

When I was little

At some point you will find it helpful to spend a lot of time talking about what it felt like to be little: 'What were your parents like?' 'What is the first thing you remember?' 'Who were you like?' 'Who were you close to?' 'Do you ever find yourself dealing with your children just like your parents dealt with you?' 'Does history repeat itself?' 'What were your parents really good at?' 'What was not so good?' 'What do you try to do differently?' perhaps more importantly: 'How do you remember feeling when this happened?' leading up to 'Do you think (child) sometimes feels like that too?'

Sometimes this reflection takes longer than one or two sessions. We also used to suggest that everyone (including therapists) bring in a photo of when they were a baby.

Who helps me

Spend time talking about the support networks available to the families. Again, this can help mothers tune in to good sources of support or, indeed, to realise that they are managing incredibly well given they have so little family help: 'Who has other family living close by?' 'Who gets help from grandparents?' 'Is this always helpful?' 'Are there problems with how your parents or parents-in-law see you as a mum?' 'What do you find helps?' 'Who has to do it alone?' 'How helpful is Dad/partner?' 'How helpful are friends?' 'What professionals or services have you tried?' 'What has helped?' 'What has not? 'Why?' Share ideas together and keep reflecting this back to feelings: 'How did you *feel* when she said *that*?' This can run over from session to session.

You might decide that many of the issues for the mothers are based on practical day-to-day problems such as shopping, tantrums or bedtimes. As such, you may decide to go away and keep diaries on what is happening and share approaches that have been helpful. This should not take over the whole course since you are working on feelings and relationships rather than behaviour management. But if you can combine the emotional side with a feeling of real success in management, it will go a long way to making family life more bearable. Sometimes you can usefully spend an entire session focusing on a topic such as tantrums and the feelings that these arouse.

My child

Once you have done some talking about the mothers' own childhoods and who they resemble, it is time to talk about their children: 'Who is he like?' 'What about her temperament?' 'Who does she remind you of?' 'What bits are like you?' Does he react the same as you?' 'Does that mean she is really very sensitive?' 'How clever that was – does she pick things up very quickly?' You can sometimes come out of this session having shed a new light on a child that will influence how a mother sees her child's behaviour.

Beware the self-fulfilling prophecy: 'He's just like his dad and he was a bad one.' Instead, steer this towards a discussion about how individual each child is and how they are always made up of bits of Mum, bits of Dad and bits of what happened to them. Take note of the blanket statement: 'She's evil' and turn this into talk about a child's behaviour instead. Sometimes, this can lead into an interesting talk about whether babies are evil or whether they simply learn to behave in certain ways because of what happens to them – in which case, they can also learn new ways of behaving if we love and help them enough.

Getting through the day

Simply talking about the typical day, what happens and the feelings generated can lead to some useful discussion about practicalities and coping. The aim in this session is to encourage mothers to share approaches and ideas, to feel proud of their own suggestions and benefit from other people's. We sometimes used a video to prompt discussion.

Lifelines

Once the group has settled, you can spend a session helping mothers draw out their own lifelines on a large sheet of paper, marking off key points in their lives. They have to feel comfortable about doing this if it is to be helpful. They then share a 'This is my life', showing off their lifelines. The important thing to remember here is that the discussion is steered towards feelings and bringing in others who have had similar experiences.

Useful strategies to share

It is helpful to have a few strategies up your sleeve for helping the sessions end on positive notes and giving the mothers a practical 'job to do'.

Supportive play

Suggest (as an experiment, perhaps) that mothers set aside 10 minutes a day for a play session with their child, returning the following week to report on how it went. They should ask their child what they wish to play with and join in wholeheartedly. They should keep up a running commentary on what they are both doing rather than shoot questions at their child. They should use praise but never criticism. They should use as much laughter and hugs as possible. And they should make this time a special time and a priority within the family day.

Using praise and rewards
Discuss the difference between a bribe (which is in the child's control) and a reward (which is the gift of the adult). Again set up an experiment where each mother tries to find 10 things each day to praise the child for, ignoring the rest as far as it is safe to do so. Teach the rules–praise–ignore approach in which you give your child clear rules, ignore silliness and praise appropriate behaviour.

1–2–3 warnings
With older children, teach mothers the skill of focusing the child's attention, giving a clear rule or instruction (just a few words with keywords emphasised in a calm, assertive tone – practise saying this!), then allowing a slow one–two–three for the child to conform. If they do, use warm praise. If they do not, *gently* lead them through what you asked them to do and praise afterwards.

Claiming stories
Help each mother invent a special bedtime story to tell her child. It will be all about how that child was when a baby and how special that child is. It will be along the lines of:

> *When you were tiny you were the most precious thing in my life. I took you home from hospital and I counted all your tiny toes. There were one, two . . . (counting the child's toes again), and your tiny hands were so soft. And you made sweet little gurgling sounds – and such a funny face sometimes that it made us all laugh. And you used to love doing . . . And one day . . . And it made me so happy when . . . (etc.)*

These 'claiming narratives' are a strong way of making a relationship closer.

Calm and consistency

Discuss the reasons for the need for calm and consistency. Link the calmness back to the mothers' own experiences of being shouted at. Point out that when we are angry we have chemicals in our body that flood into our blood. They get us ready for a good fight, but they do not allow us to think clearly. The more we shout at our children, the more we confuse them and the worse they behave. Sometimes families have patterns in which children push adults to their limits just to see how far they can go. Does this sound familiar? Children need to know where they are and how far they can go and this is where consistency comes in. Set a challenge for everyone to try to keep their cool and to return next session with one story of how pleased they were with themselves for staying calm when pushed.

Chapter 4

Relationship play time

In this chapter there are suggestions for the staff who will be leading the relationship play session for the parents or carers and their children. This play time comes at the end of the mothers' group. Mothers, therapists and observer move to another room where the children they are working with join them. Professionals observe the reuniting of parents and child in the hope that warmer greetings (and more secure separations) will develop over the course of the sessions. The relationship play time takes place in a room that has floor space for sitting in a circle and few distractions.

Activities

Ask mothers and children to sit in a circle on the floor with you. Make sure children are sitting next to or cuddled into their mother. At this point your aim is to strengthen the attachment of mother and child and not to develop a close attachment between child and one of the professionals.

Space the professionals around the circle so that each is close enough to support one or two of the families if needed. By this stage, you will have therapist, co-therapist and observer in your circle as well as the mothers. The observer is now talking and relating to the mothers and professionals again and is no longer playing an observer role. It is probable that one of these three professionals will double as the play time leader. Some groups introduce a new professional at this stage if that person is more skilled in this kind of activity.

Because of the young age of the children, the play time will only last 10 to 15 minutes – 20 minutes maximum. In the groups we ran, we based the play times on two theoretical models – the *Music Makers: Music circle times to include everyone* (Mortimer, 2006) and on the ideas from *Relationship Play* (see page 48). The aim is to start with non-threatening activities that do not place demands on a mother and child having to relate too closely. Activities tend to involve little touch and eye contact. You then progress over the sessions to activities and action rhymes that involve closer contact, more interaction, and a sharing of pleasure and fun together. The activities below are arranged in approximate order from least physical and emotional involvement to the most, so that you can dip in and choose three or four for each play time, depending on the rate at which your particular group is progressing.

Starting off

Break the ice by singing a familiar song to start with. Keep this song the same throughout the sessions. We chose *The wheels on the bus* since everyone knew it and we could vary the verses from the impersonal ('the wheels on the bus go round and round') to the more intimate ('the horn on the bus goes beep, beep, beep' with mothers gently pushing their child's nose). Towards the end of the sessions, we had 'the mums on the bus go cuddle, cuddle, cuddle' or 'tickle, tickle, tickle' and we had children pretending to be babies and cuddling into mums for 'the babies on the bus fall fast asleep'. Thus in one rhyme, you can see the whole progression of relationship play time.

Greeting

We moved on to a greeting, with the play-time leader moving around the circle singing a hello song such as: *Harry Gray, Harry Gray, where are you? Here I am, here I am, how do you do?* This started as a simple greeting from the leader with the families not being expected to provide a response. As the sessions progressed, eye contact was sought and later a wave or a handshake. Mothers and children thus progress from embarrassed ignoring to full involvement. It is important at this stage that the leader is not embarrassed, but proceeds as if everyone is delighted. It is worth the perseverance. After the greeting song, we had one or two activities or action rhymes.

Pass the parcel

Wrap up a parcel with enough layers for each child and mother pair. We had a toy in the middle that could be shared – a pack of balloons perhaps.

Start and stop a musical tape or CD and encourage a mother and child together to unwrap one layer if the parcel stops with them. Make sure everyone has a turn. Stop to share the prize or blow up balloons at the end. This activity gives parents a clear 'job to do' that is familiar and not threatening, yet does not expect them to respond emotionally to their children.

Row row
  Sing the familiar rhyme:
    Row row row your boat, gently down the stream,
    Merrily merrily merrily merrily; life is but a dream.

In the earlier sessions, children can have their backs to mothers and simply sing this in a circle as parents rock them slightly. Towards the end, we had mothers and children facing each other and sharing fun. Try changing the last line:
    If you see a crocodile, don't forget to scream!
    If you see a tall giraffe, don't forget to laugh!
    If you see a hippopotamus, don't forget to make a lot of fuss!

End with the first verse again.

Draw-around
  Towards the beginning of the 10 sessions, we set up an activity in which mothers draw around the shape of their child's hands, taking it home to colour in. Therapists would then help children draw round their mother's hands. Later on, we had the same activity but involving whole body shapes – a more personal activity than the first.

Shake up
  Mothers were asked to place their child in front of them (or cuddled into a lap). When the leader shook a tambourine, they were asked to shake their child gently all over and share the fun, stopping when the tambourine was struck again. This is repeated three or four times. Later on, they had their children facing them and shared eye contact and fun as they wobbled together.

Teamwork

Songs can be introduced that involve an element of choice and decision. For example, in *Old Macdonald had a farm* you can stop between verses to ask a mother and child pair for a suggestion for the next animal. The aim is to get mothers and children thinking and planning together.

Getting physical

Familiar rhymes can also be adapted to encourage greater physical interaction between mother and child. For example, in *Incy Wincy Spider*, the mother can creep her fingers up and down the child's arm. In *Round and round the garden*, the mother can trace her fingers gently in the palm of her child's hand. We sent home a parent song book so that mothers had the words and songs to use at home as well.

Pass the sound

Pass some jingle bells of a shaker around the circle. At first, suggest that each person makes as much noise as possible. Then pass it silently around the room. This activity requires a level of eye contact and 'tuning in' to how the next person is passing the instrument.

Heads and shoulders

In this familiar rhyme, we asked mothers to gently touch their child for the named body parts: heads, shoulders, knees, toes, etc. We started really slowly, then had a faster verse and ended with a rapid verse and a tickle at the end. You will find many more songs and activities to adapt (always moving from less personal to more physical and interactive) in *Music Makers: Music circle times to include everyone* (Mortimer, 2006).

Band time

After the first two sessions and when the group was settling in, we introduced a march at the end of the play time. We would put on some music and each carry an instrument as we marched around the room together. This activity can make mothers feel very proud of their little ones and share a lot of pleasure as they see their child's reaction. It is, therefore, a lovely activity to have towards the end of play time.

Goodbye song

At the end of play time, sing a simple and familiar 'goodbye' song to signal the end of the time. For example, *Now it's time to say goodbye, Mum and Feras, off you fly!* At this stage, mothers and children move through to the crèche to collect any other siblings. Professionals withdraw to the group room for the feedback half-hour (see page 34).

Chapter 5

Evaluation

This chapter contains suggestions for evaluation and reporting back to management committees. You have several methods to choose from when evaluating a group such as Making Connections.

Asking for feedback

You might ask the parents or carers directly about what they thought about Making Connections once their sessions are over. Here is a form that you can adapt or copy, using it either as a written questionnaire or a semi-structured interview.

Making Connections Evaluation
Confidential

Thank you for attending the group. We hope you found it useful and enjoyable. Please give us some anonymous feedback to help us plan future groups – do feel free to be open with us.

Before the group began

How did you find out about the group?

Was the information given to you: Too much?   Just right?   Too little?

Did you feel prepared for the first session?   Yes   No

Coming to the group

Did your child enjoy coming?   Yes   No

Why?

What difference has the group made:

to you?

to your child/ren?

What changes in the group do you feel are needed?

What activity did you find most useful? (Please number 1 as most useful and 3 as least)

     Talking time
     Relationship Play activity
     Other – please tell us what

Was the venue suitable?   Yes   No

Would you recommend the group to
other families?   Yes   No

Why?

Thank you for your time.
From the Making Connections Team

Attendance records

One of the simplest ways to monitor success of the group is to keep a register of attendance (assuming that each family has enrolled to receive Sure Start services) or a tally count, week by week. Families soon vote with their feet if you are not fulfilling a need. In certain situations (such as a family's moving to a different group) this can be followed up by finding out why they no longer attend.

Another method is to use observation. Usually, these observations would be objective and clear, using language that is unambiguous and unemotive. For example, you will have your week-by-week observations of how the mothers felt and responded to their children and how the meetings and greetings went following the talking time (see page 15).

Video recording of mother and child playing together (see page 23) can also reveal encouraging changes in the ways parents or carers are relating to and enjoying their children, though these involve obtaining written permissions for all the families concerned, making it clear that confidentiality will be maintained and explaining how and when the records will be used.

Reporting to management

It is helpful if you can report back to management regularly on the perceived effectiveness of the groups. One reason for this is to justify the staffing levels and resources: unless you can show that the group actually changes patterns of parenting, it might not be seen as 'value for money'. You will, therefore, find it helpful to report not only on parents' evaluations, but your own evaluations on how you feel those families will now cope and whether you feel that you have been able to work preventatively.

References

Binney, V., McKnight, I. and Broughton, S. (1994) 'Relationship Play Therapy for Attachment Disturbances in Four to Seven Year Old Children', *The Clinical Application of Ethology and Attachment Theory*, Occasional Papers No 9. Association for Child Psychology and Psychiatry.

Bowlby, J. (1988) *A Secure Base: Clinical Implications of Attachment Theory*. London: Routledge.

Holmes, J. (1993) 'Attachment Theory: A Biological Basis for Psychotherapy?' *British Journal of Psychiatry*, Volume 163, pages 430 – 438.

Mortimer, H. (2006) *Music Makers: Music circle times to include everyone*. Lichfield: QEd Publications.

Useful books

DfES (2001) *Promoting Children's Mental Health within Early Years and School Settings*. Nottingham: DfES Publications (DfES ref. 0112/2001).

Merrett, F. (1997) *Positive Parenting*. Lichfield: QEd Publications.

Mortimer, H. (2001) *Personal, Social and Emotional Development in the Early Years*. Lichfield: QEd Publications.

Mortimer, H. (2003) *Emotional Literacy and Mental Health in the Early Years*. Lichfield: QEd Publications.

Mortimer, H. (2004) *Managing Children's Behaviour*. From the 'Early Years Training and Management Series'. Leamington Spa: Scholastic.

Mortimer, H. (2005) *RUMPUS: Planning behaviour groups for parents and carers of young children*. Lichfield: QEd Publications.

Mortimer, H. (2005) *Music and Play: Introducing parents and carers of young children to working in groups*. Lichfield: QEd Publications.

Quinn, M. and T. (1995) *From Pram to Primary: Parenting small children from birth to age six or seven*. Newry: Family Caring Trust.

Sutton, C. (1999) *Helping Families with Troubled Children: A Preventative Approach*. Chichester: Wiley.

Useful resources

Early Learning Centre for tapes, instruments and song books.
Tel: 08705 352352
Website: www.elc.co.uk

Harrop, B., Friend, L. and Gadsby, D. (1975) *Okki-tokki-unga: Action Songs for Children*. London: A & C Black.

Music Education Supplies Ltd, 101 Banstead Road South, Sutton, Surrey SM2 5LH

Pavelko, V. and Scott, L.B. (1976) *Apusskidu: Songs for Children*. London: A & C Black.

Useful organisations

Barnardo's
Tanners Lane, Barkingside, Ilford, Essex IG6 1QG
Tel: 020 8550 8822   Fax: 020 8551 6870
Website: www.barnardos.org.uk
Provides care and support for children in need and their families, with projects throughout the UK. A catalogue can be obtained from Barnardo's Child Care Publications, Barnardo's Trading Estate, Paycocke Road, Basildon, Essex SS14 3DR.

Gingerbread
7 Sovereign Court, Sovereign Close, London E1W 3HW
Tel: 0800 018 4318 (freephone advice line, 10am–4pm Monday–Friday)
Fax: 020 7488 9333
Email: office@gingerbread.org.uk
Website: www.gingerbread.org.uk
Supports lone parents and their children with financial, social and legal advice, and through social and practical activities. There are over 300 local self-help groups.

National Association of Toy and Leisure Libraries
68 Churchway, London NW1 1LT
Tel: 020 7255 4600
Email: admin@playmatters.co.uk
Website: www.natll.org.uk

National Children's Bureau
8 Wakley Street, London EC1V 7QE
Tel: 020 7843 6000 or 020 7843 6008 (library enquiry line: 10am–12 noon
and 2pm–4pm)
Fax: 020 7843 6007
Email: library@ncb.org.uk
Website: www.ncb.org.uk
A multidisciplinary organisation concerned with the promotion and
identification of the interests of all children and young people. It is also
involved in research, policy and practice development, and consultancy.

National NEWPIN
Sutherland House, 35 Sutherland Square, London SE17 3EE
Tel: 020 7703 6326
Fax: 020 7701 2660
Email: newpin@nationalnewpin.freeserve.co.uk
Website: www.newpin.org.uk
Offers parents and children an opportunity to achieve positive changes in
their lives and relationships, and break the cycle of destructive family
behaviour. There are several centres, mainly in the London area. Newpin
offers parenting skills training programmes and includes a fathers' project.

Parent Network (Scotland)
15 Smith's Place, Edinburgh EH6 8NT
Tel: 0131 555 6780
Fax: 0131 555 6780
Email: info@parentnetwork.demon.co.uk
A programme of information, education and support run by trained parents
for parents.

Parentline Plus
529 Highgate Studios, 53–79 Highgate Road,
London NW5 1TL
Tel: 020 7284 5500   Parentline: 0808 800 2222
Fax: 020 7584 55021
Email: headoffice@parentlineplus.org.uk
Website: www.parentlineplus.org.uk

PIPPIN Parents in Partnership – Parent Infant Network
Derwood, Todds Green, Stevenage, Herts SG1 2JE
Tel: 01438 748487
Fax: 01438 748182
Website: www.pippin.org.uk
This national charity, which promotes positive early family and parent-infant relationships, aims to maintain and improve the emotional health of families during the period surrounding the birth of a new baby. It offers parentcraft classes, and a range of projects which include work with fathers.